This book is dedicated to those men and women who began the quest to explore our universe, and to those children who will someday continue the journey.

The author wishes to thank Dr. Richard C. Jones for his cosmic advice.

The author also thanks Bruce T. Draine, Professor of Astrophysical Sciences, Princeton University Observatory, for reading this book prior to its publication.

ISBN 0-590-48825-2

Copyright © 1993 by Loreen Leedy.
All rights reserved. Published by Scholastic Inc., 555 Broadway, New York, NY 10012, by arrangement with Holiday House, Inc.

12 11 10 9 8   0/0

Printed in the U.S.A.   14

First Scholastic printing, January 1995

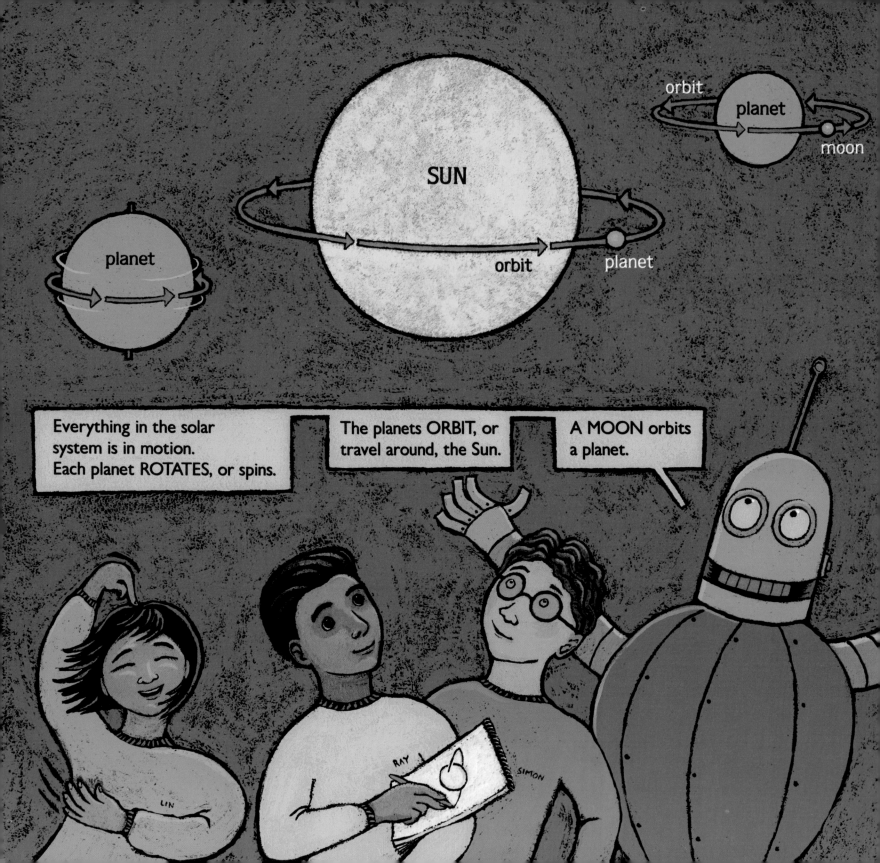

First we'll fly by the biggest, hottest, brightest object in the solar system—the Sun.

Dear Mom & Dad,
 Did U know that R
Sun is really a ☆?
It is only a medium-
sized ☆, but over 1
million Earths could
fit inside. We can't 🐝
2 close because of the
intense heat (millions
of degrees!)
 Stay cool- Your ☀
 Ray

P.S. The Sun has darker, cooler blotches called SUNSPOTS.

SOLAR ECLIPSE

Mr.+Mrs. Sol Corona
93 Shady Lane
Sun Valley, Idaho
U.S.A.   83353

I am a STAR!

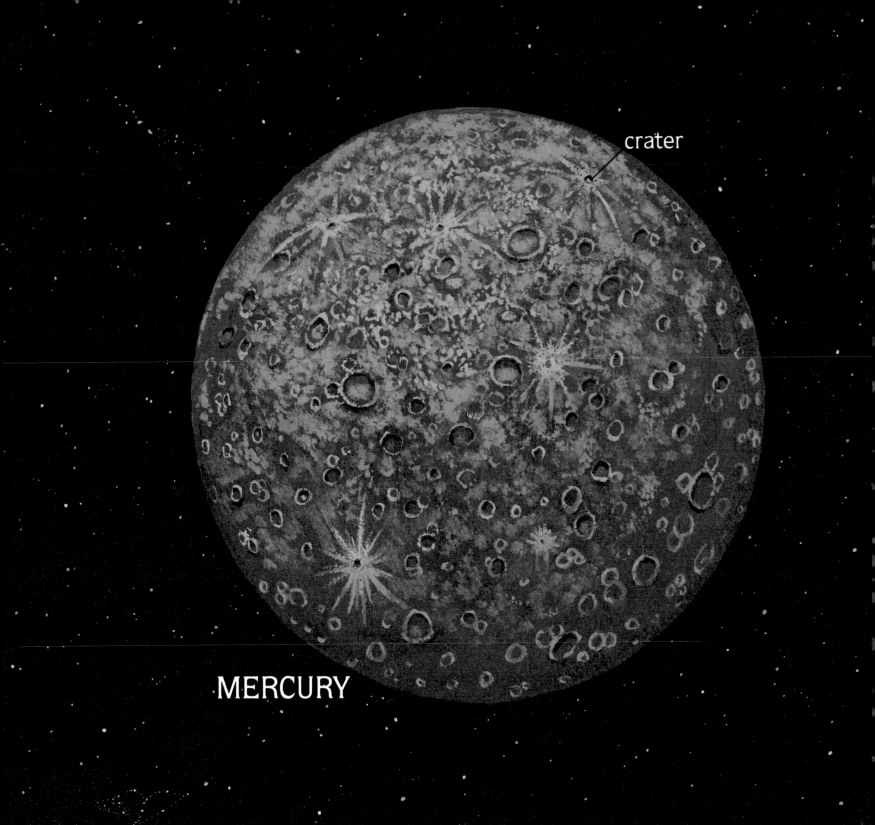

crater

MERCURY

Dear Debbie,
  We saw Venus today, and it's a little smaller than Earth, but much more dangerous. It is covered with thick, poisonous, acid clouds. The air has enough heat and pressure to crack spaceships! Venus has lots of earsplitting thunder, and lightning, too.
  Wish you were here!
    Your friend,
    Simon

Debbie DeMilo
201 Flytrap St.
Cupid City, NY
12420

VENUS

EARTH

Dear Mom,
    Guess what? We saw the actual footprints of the first astronaut to walk on Earth's moon~Neil Armstrong. We left our footprints, too.   They'll last forever because there's no wind or rain to destroy them. I guess a meteor might crash down on them. That's how the moon's craters were made. I hope a meteor doesn't land on <u>us</u>!
                        Love,
                          Tanisha
P.S. On Earth I weigh 72 pounds—here I weigh only 12!

Luna Cee
100 Crescent Ave.
Crater Lake, OR
U.S.A. 97604

meteor

OUCH!

MOON

Earth

MARS

Dear Uncle Martin,
  Here is a poem about Mars~
  RED PLANET
  Canyons,
  Volcanoes,
  Clouds of dust,
  Boulders,
  Craters,
  The color of rust.
Scientists think Mars
used to have water in
rivers or oceans. It still
has ice at the poles, but
it's a desert planet now.
  See you!   Love,
           Lin

P.S. Mars has 2
small moons.

Mr. Martin Greenman
#4 Canal Street
Venice, FL
U.S.A.   33595

PHOBOS
DEIMOS

I am so
thirsty!

Look at the thousands of asteroids we're passing. The asteroid belt is between the small, rocky inner planets and the giant outer planets.

ASTEROID

Dear Mom and Dad,

Dr. Quasar says that asteroids are big chunks of rock. Most of them stay in the asteroid belt, but one could drift out of orbit and crash into a planet (even Earth!)

Love,

Simon

Mr. and Mrs. Goldbloom
1000 Collision Road
Bumpers, NJ
U.S.A. 08857

P.S. Don't bother wearing helmets - the chance of an asteroid hitting Earth is very small.

JUPITER is made of gases and liquids that swirl around. It has the GREAT RED SPOT which is really a huge storm.
Dear Stella,
Did U know that Jupiter is the BIGGEST planet? It has colorful stripes, + a very faint ring system made of dust. think the weirdest thing is that has no solid crust of land. Maybe it is sort of like melted ! C U later... Your bro,
Ray
P.S. has 16 's.
Stella Corona
93 Shady Lane
Sun Valley, Idaho
U.S.A. 83353
1st

JUPITER

SATURN'S hundreds of rings look solid from a distance, but they are made mostly of many small pieces of ice.

Dear Mom and Dad,
  Here is a poem for you~
SATURN'S RINGS
Snowballs
And icebergs
Drifting in space
Around the planet
The icy chunks race.

I think Saturn is the prettiest planet. It has more than 20 moons (scientists keep finding new ones!) Love, Lin

Mr. and Mrs. Chang
808 Circle Court
Loopdeloop, CA
U.S.A.   90287

SATURN

Most planets orbit the Sun upright, but URANUS lies on its side.

Dear Grandpa & Grandma,
   Uranus is the tilted planet. It looks like a spinning top that fell down. Scientists think a big asteroid could have knocked it over. The whole planet is covered by a thick, blue-green fog. Uranus has rings, just like the other gas giant planets. Also, it has 15 known moons.
   I miss you! Love,
                Tanisha

Mr. and Mrs. Lean
507 Topple St.
Sideways, MI
U.S.A. 48756

Hi!

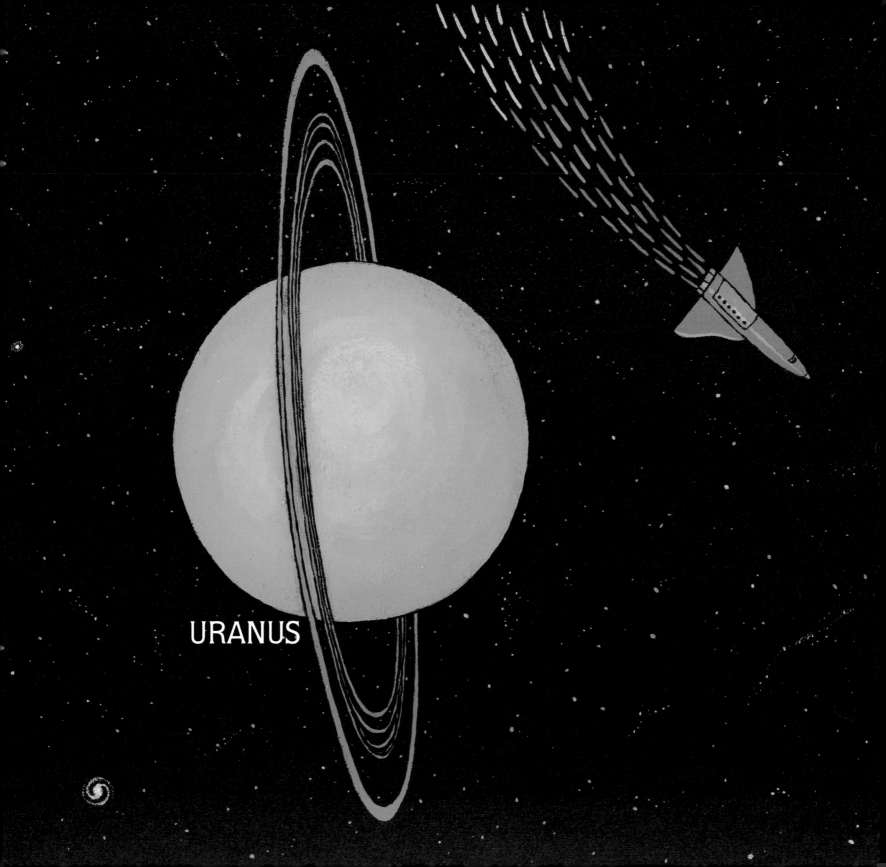

URANUS

NEPTUNE

Dear Grandfather,
Can you believe it-
we are 6 billion kilometers
from home! Pluto is the
very smallest planet, and
the last one in the solar
system (as far as we know.)
Scientists think another
planet could be hiding out
here. Maybe when I grow
up, I'll discover it!
See you soon- Love,
MINDA

Joe Thunderhawk
248 Final Trail
Tail End, TX
U.S.A. 77050

P.S. Pluto has one big moon, called Charon.

PLUTO

Charon

It's time to head back to Earth. I hope you all enjoyed your tour of the solar system.
Dear Mom + Dad,
Here R some of the
space words learned:
ASTEROID- space rock
COMET- chunk of frozen gas & dust
CRATER- circular hollow
GALAXY- huge group of stars
MOON- it orbits a planet
ORBIT- to travel around
PLANET- it orbits a star
ROTATE- to spin
STAR- it gives off heat and light
want to visit another galaxy next, okay? ♡, Ray
Mr. + Mrs. Sol Corona
93 Shady Lane
Sun Valley, ID
U.S.A. 83353